THE RIDICULOUSLY SIMPLE GUIDE TO FINAL CUT PRO X

A BEGINNERS GUIDE TO VIDEO EDITING LIKE A PRO

RYAN DOUGLAS

Minute Help Press
ANAHEIM, CALIFORNIA

Contents

About Minute Help

Minute Help Press is building a library of books for people with only minutes to spare. Follow @minutehelp on Twitter to receive the latest information about free and paid publications from Minute Help Press, or visit minutehelp.com.

DISCLAIMER

This book is not endorsed by Apple and should be considered unofficial.

[1]

INTRODUCTION

Apple promises that Final Cut – the company's flagship digital editing software – is "not just a different cut, but a whole new production" – and it truly is. Workflow is faster, smoother and easier than ever. Background tasks are completely automated, and with the program logistics under control, you're free to fully explore your creativity.

New Features

A significant departure from previous versions, Final Cut X is redesigned for the continued evolution of cloud-based digital movie editing and collaboration. Robust assistant editor capacities help organize projects and media better than any existing editing software system. Final Cut X is not merely an upgrade from 7, but a completely new and faster digital editing program that harnesses the power of OS X in new and exciting ways. Here are just a few of the new features:

- Uninterrupted editing. With Final Cut 7, rendering halted the editing process. This is no longer the case; rendering, importing and even analyzing and fixing tasks occur in the background without interpreting your editing flow.
- Improved ingest. Final Cut Pro automatically controls for quality, stabilization, image color and audio cleanup during the importation process. Plus, you can begin organizing footage immediately using metadata keywords and smart collections based on people recognition and shot detection.

- Magnetic timeline. Audio and video are locked in sync, making it virtually impossible to accidentally separate the two.

Tech Specs

Final Cut Pro is completely re-engineered to support 64-bit processing. What does this mean for you? With 64-bit processing, your Mac is now a multi-tasking master, and Final Cut Pro takes full advantage of this enhanced power. Just like how transmission gears determine how fast a car can go, the number of bits (in this case 64) determines how quickly a computer can process information. With 64-bit processing, everything runs faster, so Final Cut can quickly process a variety of video formats from DV to 4K, instantly color-correct video, and deftly handle large project sand sequences. Final Cut is built on the Apple Cocoa framework, which means it is an OS-X native application. Why does this matter? The older versions of Final Cut evolved from Macromedia, and consequently lacked much of Apple's intuitive interface and user-friendly features. By utilizing the familiar interface elements and technologies we already know and love, Cocoa makes Final Cut naturally user-friendly, intuitive and interactive – just like its little sister, iMovie.

Final Cut Pro X introduces new features, including media stems export, Xsan projects and events for multi-users, and rich XML support, which make Final Cut Pro even more flexible and compatible. Enhanced media organization makes it easy to find clips, "auditions" let you sample different clips to choose the perfect shot, and the inline precision editor allows for precise audio and visual adjustments. Transition and effects are also easy. For example, a simple keyboard shortcut allows for the most popular effect, cross dissolve – there's no need to search for it in the effects library. And thanks to the ability to customize all your keyboard shortcuts, your most-used transitions can all be a keystroke away.

However, since Final Cut Pro X is, in essence, version one of a software program, it is not without its flaws. Think of Final Cut X as an entirely new program that simply kept the name, but changed many of the fundamentals. For example, one of the biggest problems with Final Cut X is that it cannot open Final Cut 7 projects (see 3.1 for a workaround). Apple has corrected other issues, such as the inability to relink missing media, with updated releases of Final Cut Pro X. Users are encouraged to contact Apple support with requests for added features.

This guide will help users who are completely new to Final Cut and movie editing get started. We'll also explain how to import old projects from iMovie (sadly, there's no backwards compatibility for Final Cut Pro 7), master the new interface and put the power of Final Cut Pro X to work for video production. For users who are switching over from Final Cut 7, we'll make the transition process as smooth as possible.

[2]

GETTING STARTED: FINAL CUT OVERVIEW

2.1 Final Cut Interface

If you are familiar with iMovie or have used older versions of Final Cut Pro, you will be right at home with the Final Cut Pro X interface. When you launch Final Cut Pro for the first time, an empty interface will appear. Just like iMovie and older Final Cut versions, there are three key windows in Final Cut:

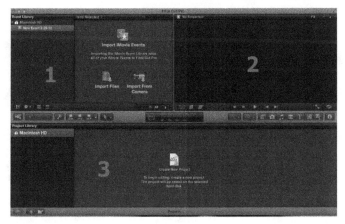

1. Event Browser: Access and organize source media files

2. Viewer: Play back clips and projects

3. Magnetic Timeline: Add and arrange clips on this magnetic storyboard to create your movie; clips "magnetically" adjust to fill/create space as new clips are added/removed

Event Browser:

1. Hide/Reveal Event Library

2. Event Browser: View and sort clips within the selected Event

Clip Viewer:

1. Onscreen controls: manage effects including transform, crop and rotate

2. Playback controls

3. Full-screen playback: toggle in/out of full screen mode

Magnetic Timeline:

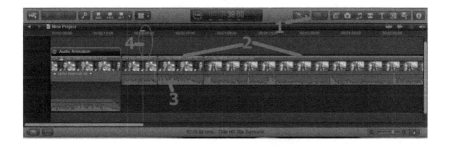

1. Toolbar
2. Primary Storyline
3. Audio Clips
4. Playhead: a gray, vertical line that marks your current position within the Timeline. Move the playhead to scrub or switch back and forth between different locations.

2.2 Media Files and Clips

Final Cut Pro uses non-destructive editing. This means that any changes you make during the editing process are only made to the Final Cut Pro clips, and not the actual media files.

What is a media file?

A media file is typically a video, although it can also be an audio, still image or graphics file that you import into Final Cut. Since media files are quite large, they typically are stored on external drives.

What is a clip?

A clip represents the source media file. These clips live inside the Events folder (see 2.3). In technology jargon, we say that a clip "points to" or "links to" a media file. This means you can modify a clip without changing the actual media file. Any edits you make to a clip are only reflected within the Events folder where that specific clip lives. Trimming or deleting parts of a clip removes the clip from your Events folder, but not from source media files.

2.3 Events

In Final Cut Pro, just like Apple's iLife programs, imported media is categorized as Events, which are stored in the Event Library. Think of an Event as a container for your clip files. You can group Events by date, theme, subject and more. A white-starred purple icon identifies events. To show or hide the event library, click on the Show/Hide button on the Tool bar, or go to Window -> Show/Hide Event Library. To create a new Event, go to File -> New Event or use the keyboard shortcut Option + N.

2.4 Final Cut 7 to Final Cut X: Transition Tips

While Final Cut X is new, powerful program, many of the same fundamental techniques are similar to Final Cut 7. However, the nomenclature has dramatically changed. Here's how to make sense of the different terms used in this guide.

What is the difference between projects/sequences in Final Cut 7 and projects/events in Final Cut x?

Final Cut 7 and Final Cut X use different terms for similar concepts. In Final Cut 7, a project contained both the sequences of editing decisions as well as your clips that are connected to the source files. In Final Cut X, editing information is stored separately from media information. Multiple projects in Final Cut X may contain the same media. Projects may be organized within the Project Library by using folders.

What happens to my media when I import it into Final Cut X?

When you import media, it becomes associated with an Event. Events contain clips (the media) and are organized within the Events folder. Multiple clips and events can be shared between different projects. In Final Cut 7, users had to set a scratch disk location to store video and audio files upon import. Another location was also required for render files, such as thumbnails and audio waveforms. This is no longer the case in Final Cut X. All project information is stored within the project folder. All the render files are stored within a Project subfolder. This means you can easily move files to different locations without losing any information.

How do I customize shortcut commands?

In Final Cut 7, commands and the keyboard layout were managed through Tools -> Keyboard Layout -> Customize. Commands are now managed through the Command Editor. Go to Final Cut -> Commands -> Customize.

How do I organize and edit my media?

Final Cut 7 and Final Cut X use similar organization and editing fundamentals, although these techniques are now called different names. Here's a cheat list:

Final Cut 7	Final Cut X
Item Properties	Inspector
Bins	Keyword Collections
Subclips	Range-based keywords
Markers	Favorites
Tracks	Storylines and connected clips
Nested sequences	Compound clips
Linked clips	*n/a, video and audio are a single combined unit*
Merged clips	Synchronized clips
Multiclips	Multicam clips

[3]

IMPORTING FILES

Final Cut Pro makes it easy to import files from a digital, SLR or 4K camera, as well as film, iMovie still photos and MP3 files. Plus, with Final Cut Pro X, you can start editing before you've even finished your import. Simply select what you want to import and how you want to do it, and Final Cut Pro manages all the background tasks of organizing, repairing and optimizing your media.

3.1 Importing files: the basics

Final Cut supports direct importation of files as well as importation of streaming DV capture via FireWire or video captured via third-party video cards. In general, follow these steps for importing media:

1. To import files directly into an event, first select your event.
2. Next, click the Import Files button on the Event Browser and select File -> Import.
3. If you don't see the Event Library, click the Event Library button from the lower-left corner of the Event Browser.

4. Choose between importing files or importing directly from your connected camera.

5. To import more than one clip at the same time, simply click the first clip and shift+click to select the last; every clip that's in between will also be selected.

When importing files, you can choose to either copy the original files or to create an alias of the files. If you deselect the "Copy files to Final Cuts Events folder", then only an alias pointing back to the original files will be created. While this saves on disc storage space, if you ever delete or move the original files, Final Cut will no longer be able to locate them.

How do I import video from my digital camera?

If you are importing video files from a photo-based device (e.g., your standard point-and-shoot digital camera), you will need to import the video directly from the memory card, rather than simply plugging the camera into the computer. To do so, use an SD card reader and navigate to the memory card's video folder. Select the desired files and follow the instructions above.

NOTE: If you import video first directly to iPhoto or Aperture, these files will not appear in the Final Cut library until you add them. To do so, simply select the files and then drag and drop them into a Final Pro Event folder.

How do I import files from a tape-based recording device?

Final Cut Pro can import files from a camcorder or other tape-based device.

1. Attach the camcorder to the computer
2. Turn on the camcorder and set it to VTR or VCR mode
3. From Final Cut Pro, go to File -> Import from Camera
4. The Camera Import Window will appear; an image is displayed showing the tape's current position
5. If you wish to start importing from a different location, use the playback

control keys to set your tape and click Import

6. Choose how to organize your clips: either add them to an existing Event or create a new Event

7. Choose whether you wish to transcode your media, analyze for audio problems or analyze for video problems; click Import

8. The video will play as it is imported; the import process moves at the same speed that the video plays

9. Importing will stop when the tape reaches the end or when you select 'Stop Import'

Can I use my Final Cut 7 files?

Technically, Apple does not support Final Cut 7 to Final Cut Pro X. However, the app 7toX ($9.99) by Assisted Editing will convert the files to Final Cut X projects. Achieving a perfect translation is not possible, but 7toX comes pretty close, and even marks changes that occurred during conversion with "to do" markers for follow up.

3.2 Organize and edit during import

During import, Final Cut Pro can automatically identify/organize clips by face, identify shakiness, automatically balance color, and create a Keyword Collection when importing clips from a specified folder. Final Cut Pro transcodes media to optimize for better editing, color quality and rendering. Transcoding copies your media files while preserving the originals. Here's how to get started:

- **Identify/Organize by Face:** Activate the "Find People" option to analyze images and create a Keyword Collection based on the number of people in each shot as well as the type of shot. After import, you will have the following collections: One Person, Two Persons, Group, Close Up, Medium Shot, Wide Shot.
- **Balance Color:** From the Toolbar, select the Inspector button. Click the

Video tab and select 'Balance'. This enables the color balance effect.

- **Identify Shakiness:** Select the "Analyze for Stabilization and Rolling Shutter" option on import. Final Cut Pro will analyze each clip for stabilization issues and assign a keyword to any clip with excessive shaking.

- **Create Keywords:** Activate the "Import folders as Keyword Collections" option from the Import dialog. This will create a Keyword Collection for each imported media folder.

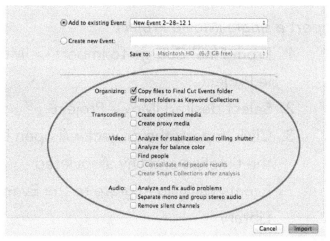

During import, choose to analyze for stabilization, color balance, facial recognition, fix audio

problems, and stereo groups. Choosing these options on import will still allow you to immediately use the clips (the analysis and editing will occur in the background without slowing down Final Cut) and will save time later when finishing your movie.

3.3 Importing from iMovie to Final Cut

Use iMovie to create a rough cut and finish the job in Final Cut Pro, or upgrade your old movies with Final Cut's precision editing. Either way, iMovie projects and files transfer seamlessly. Here's how:

Import a single iMovie Project

1. From Final Cut, go to Import -> iMovie Project
2. Select desired iMovie Project
3. Click Import; the project will open in the timeline and any associated Events will also migrate to the Event Library

NOTE: If you have an iMovie Trailer, you will first need to convert this trailer to a project before import.

Import entire iMovie Event Library
1. From Final Cut, go to Import -> iMovie Event Library
2. Click OK
3. Events from iMovie will now appear in the Final Cut Pro Event Library

3.4 Importing layered Photoshop graphics

Import layered Photoshop graphics and Final Cut will maintain the integrity of each layer. Animate, colorize and add special effects to individual layers. Each layer is treated as a separate but connected clip in the Timeline. Before import, follow these best practices:

- Create files with 8-bit RGB mode: NOTE: CMYK, Lab Color and Bitmap are NOT supported
- Create layered graphic files using a frame size compatible with TV or film

pixels; Photoshop has presets for this
compatibility

- Flatten any adjustment layers prior to import
- Verify that the desired layers are visible
- Final Cut supports embedded color; save layered files with the desired color profile

3.5 Creating camera archives

Rather than going through an entire import process, you can also use Final Cut Pro to archive the contents of your camera. (NOTE: media must be pre-recorded; you cannot archive a live video stream). This allows you to quickly empty the contents of your camera, freeing up space for reuse, while protecting and preserving the original versions of your media. Archiving also saves the media in your camera's data structure, which makes it easier to store and access files.

How do I create an archive from a file-based camera?

1. Connect the camera to your computer and set it to PC Connect mode or PC transfer mode (name may vary based on camera; consult your owners manual)
2. In Final Cut Pro, select the 'Import from Camera' button at the far left of the toolbar
3. Rather than clicking 'Import', select 'Create Archive'
4. Enter a name for your camera archive and select a location to save the archive; we recommend selecting an external drive or partitioning your existing drive
5. The archive will be stored as if it were a hard disk that can be mounted; whenever your external disk is connected to the computer, Final Cut Pro will show the mounted archive under "Camera Archives"

How do I create an archive from a tape-based camera?

1. Follow the above steps to connect your camera to the computer and open the import dialog; you must connect using a FireWire cable and not a USB cable

2. Select 'Create Camera Archive', select a location and enter a name

3. Once you click OK, Final Cut Pro will begin to play the tape, archiving from its current location

4. If you wish the archiving process to be elsewhere, use the playback controls to select the location

5. Archiving will continue until the tape comes to an end or you click "Stop Import"

[4]

ORGANIZING & SEARCHING FOR FILES

From your iPhone to your camera, the explosion of affordable HD recording devices has led to a similar explosion of HD video. Here's how to get organized and find the hidden gems in your massive amounts of HD media.

4.1 Organization basics

Event holds related media clips; these can be audio, video, or still images. As we discussed in Section 3, when you import media, you will create a new Event and give that Event a name. As with any organization system, it's only as good as the labels! We suggest giving Events a meaningful name. Depending on the amount of media clips you have, this may be as simple as "My Best Friend's Wedding" or as involved as "Rehearsal Dinner", "Ceremony", "Reception Part 1", etc. You can change these names at any time, as well as separate or merge existing folders or create a new folder.

How do I view my media clips?

Before you start organizing, you need to know what you are organizing. There are two primary ways to view clips: either in filmstrip view or list view. You can switch between either view mode by selecting either the Filmstrip or List view buttons from the bottom left of the Event Browser menu.

Filmstrip View: All clips associated with an event are displayed as thumbnails; this is useful for locating a specific clip.

TIP: To adjust filmstrip height, click the "Clip Appearance" button in the bottom right corner of the Event Browser menu.

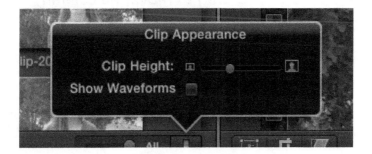

List View: Displays a list of clips and specific information associated with each clip. This information includes duration, date of import, keywords, rating, etc. You can also access different points along the filmstrip for partial or full playback.

TIP: *To customize the information display, right click on any column heading and choose a category option; to rearrange category order, simply click and drag to move the column heading to a new position.*

How can I sort clips using Event Browser?

1. Select the Event with clips you wish to sort

2. To group clips by a specific category, select the "Choose Group Clips By" option fro the Action pop-up menu at the bottom of the Event Library

3. To set the order of clips in the Event, select the "Choose Arrange Clips By" option from the Action pop-up menu

4.2 Rating clips

Not every clip contains useful content. If part of a clip has blurry or unsuitable material, you can rate this clip as "Rejected". On the other hand, if the clip perfectly captures the action, you can rate this clip as "Favorite". When you're ready to create your final cut, you can hide "rejected" clips or choose only to display "favorite" clips.

How do I rate a clip?

From the Event Browser, select the clip you wish to rate. If you love the clip, click the Favorite button from the toolbar (the green star) or press the F keyboard shortcut. If you dislike the clip, click the reject button (the red "x") or press the Delete keyboard shortcut. A green line (favorite) or red line (rejected) will also appear at the top of the clip.

How do I hide/view rated clips?

To hide rejected clips or view favorite clips, use the Filter pop-up menu, which is located at the top of the Event Browser.

How do I remove a rating?

1. First, select the clip; if it is hidden due to its rating, you may need to select the "All Clips" option from the Filter pop-up menu
2. Click the "clear rating" button from the toolbar (the clear star) or press the U keyboard shortcut.

4.3 Keywords and clips

Rather than hunting through hundreds of clips in different events, add keywords to quickly locate the clips you need. For example, let's say that you are creating a wedding video. You may wish to tag clips with keywords like "bride close-up", "groom close-up", "wedding party group shot" etc. This adds a useful level of organization to your existing Event Folders. Now you can easily find all the close-up shots of the bride, no matter which event (rehearsal dinner, ceremony, reception, etc.) holds these clips.

How do I add keywords?

You can add keywords to an entire clip, or just a portion of the clip. Here's how:

1. Use the Event Browser to open your Event and select the desired clip
2. Select either the entire clip, or click and drag to select a limited portion of the clip
3. Click the keyword (key) button on the toolbar

4. Using the Keyword Editor, enter the name or phrase for your new keyword (e.g., "bride close-up")

5. You can add multiple keywords and phrases to either the entire clip, the same selection or different selections

6. When you are finished adding keywords to the clip, close the Keyword Editor

7. If you will be adding a lot of keywords to a large number of clips, use the keyboard shortcuts to automate the process

8. Assign keyboard shortcuts by clicking the disclosure triangle to the left of the Keyword Shortcuts; keyword keyboard shortcuts are assigned to the numbers 1 through 9.

9. To use the keyboard shortcut, select either a range, one clip or multiple clips and hit the corresponding number (1 through 9)

How do I remove keywords?

1. Select the clip or range from which you wish to remove the keywords

2. A blue bar will appear at the top of the clip indicating that keywords are applied to this clip or range

3. Choose Mark -> Remove All Keywords or simply use the keyword keyboard control "0".

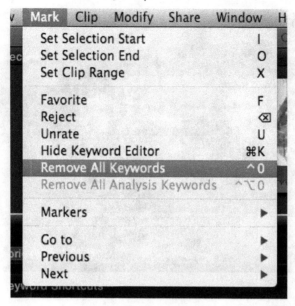

4.4. Searching and Smart Collections

Once you've assigned keywords, ratings and other criteria to your clips, use Final Cut Pro's search function to find the perfect clip for each scene. When you find what you need, save your search as a Smart Collection, which will automatically update its clip contents every time you add new clips to your Event Library.

How do I perform a search?

You can search by a combination of criteria, including rating and keyword, using the Filter Pop-Up menu.

1. From the Event Library, select the Event or folder that you wish to search

2. Click the search button located at the top of the Event Browser

3. In the filter window, add search criteria (known as "rules") by clicking the "Add Rule pop-up menu" button on the far right

4. You can add the following rules: Text, Ratings, Media Type, Stabilization, Keywords, People, Format Info, Date, Roles

5. Choose "Any" to specify that a clip must match at least one of the search criteria

6. Choose "All" to specify that a clip must match all of the search criteria

How do I create a Smart Collection?

Any search that you perform can be saved as a smart collection. Here's how to create one:

1. From the Event Library, select an Event
2. Use the Filter window to conduct your search based on the above directions
3. After you've conducted your search, click the "New Smart Collection" button in the Filter window
4. An untitled Smart Collection will appear in your Event Library
5. Enter the name for this collection
6. Any time you add clips to the Event Library with criteria matching your previous search, these clips will auto-

matically be added to the Smart Collection

7. To edit the filter criteria associated with a Smart Collection, simply select the collection from the Event Library, double click the name, and edit the criteria from within the Filter window

NOTE: If you edit the keywords, ratings or other criteria associated with a clip so that this clip no longer matches the Smart Collection's criteria, then the clip will no longer appear in the Smart Collection

4.5 Organizing clips by roles

A role is a metadata text label that Final Cut Pro automatically assigns upon import. There are five default roles: Video, Titles, Dialogue, Music and Effects.

How do I view or reassign roles?

1. From the Timeline index, click the Roles button

2. Select or deselect the roles you wish to activate or turn off

3. Active roles will appear in color on the timeline, inactive roles will appear gray.

How do I create custom roles?

1. Select a clip from the Event Browser or Timeline

2. Open the Role editor and select Modify -> Edit Roles

3. Choose the role type (either Audio Role or Video Role)

4. Enter a name for the new role

[5]

EDITING CLIPS

5.1 Creating your first project

To create a movie and begin editing your video files in Final Cut, you will first need to create a project. A project is a record of your editing and any media you use. When you create a project, you also generate a Timeline. Add visual and audio clips to your timeline, special effects, rearrange these clips and – ta da! – you are now a movie producer!

1. Start your project. Go to File -> New Project or from the Project Library, click the "New Project" button

2. Enter a name for your project

3. Select a default event for your project; if you add or drag media files directly onto the Timeline, these files will be added to the project's default Event file

4. By default, the project's timeline will begin at 00:00:00:00; if you need a different time, type that into the Starting Timecode field

5. Click OK; the new project appears in the project field and you can get started producing your movie!

NOTE: Do you need to change a project's default Event, properties or name? You can do so at any time by going to the Project Inspector button (hit the "i" button on the toolbar if this is hidden), select properties, and then select the tool to edit the properties

5.2 Adding clips to create a filmstrip

Clips are the building blocks of your movie. Adding different clips to create a story is fundamental to your movie's creation. A five-minute filmstrip may incorporate hundreds of short, two to three second clips, showing the same scene from different angles, switching between wide vs. close-up shots, and highlighting different actors in the scene.

As you build your project, your video clips will appear as a filmstrip. Running underneath your filmstrip are audio effects and music. The audio soundtrack will appear in blue. You can learn more about adding, editing and managing audio in Chapter 6.

NOTE: When managing a lot of clips, the Timeline can start to get crowded. To make more Timeline space available for viewing and editing, you can minimize clips with a specific assigned role. When minimized, these clips will appear smaller on the Timeline. This is a great way to focus specifically on the clips or special effects that you are editing.

1. From the Timeline Index, click the Roles button

2. In the Roles pane, click the Minimize button next to the role whose clips you want to minimize

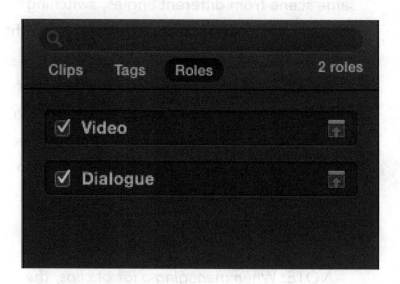

How do I select a clip?

1. To add a clip to your filmstrip, open the Event associated with the filmstrip
2. Click the clip once to select it (a yellow border will appear around the clip)
3. Drag and drop it into the Timeline

5.3 Cutting and trimming clips

How do I cut a clip on the Timeline?

1. Select 'Blade' from the Timeline tools menu or go to Edit -> Blade

2. Move the skimmer to the beginning of the frame that you wish to cut and click

3. The clip will now be divided into two clips based on where you clicked

How do I cut multiple clips at once?

You can also use the blade tool to cut both the primary storyline clips and the connected clips. Connected clips are used for cutaway shots, superimposed or composited images.

1. From the Timeline, select the clips you wish to cut; in this case, you'll need to select both the primary storyline and connected clips
2. Move the skimmer to the beginning of the frame that you wish to cut and click
3. Select Edit -> Blade
4. The selected clips will be cut at the skimmer position

How do I extend or shorten a clip?

To extend or shorten a clip, also known as "trimming" a clip, adjust the start point or end point. By default, Final Cut Pro uses the "ripple trim". This means that any adjustments to the clip's start point or end point are made without creating a gap. The adjustment "ripples out", so all subsequent clips are moved upwards or backwards.

1. From the Timeline, use the pointer tool to drag the end points and start points
2. As you drag, this will shorten or lengthen the clip
3. A numerical time code field at the top indicates how much time is being cut or added from the clip
4. When the clip is extended to its full, maximum length (i.e., all the potential footage in the clip is now included), the clip edge will turn red; this means it cannot be extended farther

How do I remove content from the beginning or end of the clip?

Oftentimes, the start or end of a clip contains information that does not need to be included in the project. To remove this content (known as a top or tail edit), there's no need for fancy editing; a quick click will get the job done.

1. Position the skimmer where you wish the clip to begin or end
2. To trim the top, go to Edit -> Trim Start
3. To trim the tail, go to Edit -> Trim End
4. The clip will automatically trim anything before or after the skimmer (depending on the type of trim) and update the Timeline accordingly with a "ripple" effect through all the existing content
5. If there are connected clips, Final Cut Pro will trim either the selected clip or the topmost clip; these rules hold true for both the primary or connected clips

5.4 Auditioning Clips

Not sure which clip is right for your movie? Use Final Pro's audition feature to try them out! You can create auditions using both the Event Browser and the Timeline. When you create an audition, you can group related clips or even use multiple versions of the same clip to try out different shot angles, treatments or titles.

How do I create an Event Browser audition?
1. Select the clips you wish to include
2. Choose Clip -> Audition -> Create (Command + Y)
3. A "spotlight" icon will appear in the upper left corner of the clip indicating that it is part of an audition

How do I create a Timeline audition?
1. To create an audition with related clips, drag a group of these clips from the Event Browser onto an existing clip on the Timeline
2. Just like with an Event Browser audition, a "spotlight" icon will appear in

the upper left corner to indicate the clip is part of an audition

3. Choose 'Add to Audition' to create an audition with the currently selected clip

How do I review clips to make a pick?

1. From the Timeline, select the audition and open it (Command + Y)
2. The audition window now appears; a "blue spotlight" will shine on the currently selected clip
3. Press the spacebar to play this clip

4. To view an alternative clip, use the right or left arrows or swipe through to a different clip
5. To finalize your choice, go to Clip -> Audition -> Finalize Audition
6. The audition will dissolve, leaving your selected clip in the Timeline
7. If you added keywords or other meta information to the audition, your selected clip will retain this information

[6]

AUDIO EDITING

Final Cut Pro will automatically analyze and enhance audio to correct common problems, including noise and hum. The app can easily add audio effects to different clips, automatically synchronize video and audio clips, and match audio between two different clips. Even better, you'll use the same tools for audio editing, like transitions, that you already use for film editing.

6.1 Adding music, narration and audio effects

"Sweetening" is the process of adding audio effects – music and sound effects – to truly bring a scene to life. After all, what would Rocky's run up the Philadelphia Art Museum's steps be without the music swelling in the background? Create your own memorable moments by adding music and audio effects, or record your own narration.

How do I add audio to a clip?

You can add music, special effects or other audio directly from iTunes or from your computer. Final Cut Pro offers an audio library with over 1,000 royalty-free music and sound effects.

1. To get started, click the music/audio button on the Timeline toolbar

2. From the pop-up browser, choose a source folder like iTunes or the Final Cut Pro library

3. Locate your audio file; to search for your file, type directly into the search field

iTunes library

Audio effects library

1. To preview an audio file, double click the file and select the 'Play' button
2. To add multiple files, command click each item
3. Drag your audio files to their desired spot on the Timeline

How do I record audio?

Using a direct input device, such as a built-in microphone, you can record audio directly through Final Cut. This function is especially useful when adding voiceover narration.

1. Position the playhead where the audio will correspond with the clip
2. Go to Window -> Record Audio

3. Adjust settings, such as input device or input channels, as necessary

4. Click the record button to begin recording

5. Click the record button a second time to stop recording, or press the spacebar

6. The audio recording will now be attached to the primary storyline, starting at the playhead position

6.2 Fading, adjusting and copying audio effects

How do I create audio fades?

The easiest way to transition from one audio clip to another is by creating a crossfade. There are three main ways to create audio fades with Final Cut Pro.

1. Automatic Crossfades during transitions: If you add a transition to your clip, Final Cut Pro will automatically apply a crossfade to any audio that is attached to this clip.

2. Crossfades: Create your own crossfades when trimming clips by applying crossfade to the edit point.

3. Fade handles: Create fade-ins and fade-outs by selecting two adjacent clips on the timeline
   - Go to Clip -> Expand Audio/Video
   - Drag the audio portions of the clips so they overlap
   - Drag the fade handles of each clip to the point where the fade will begin

- Change the fade shape by right-clicking on the fade handle and selecting between linear (constant fade rate), S-curve (ease out with midpoint at 0 dB), +3dB (start quickly, taper out slowly), or -3dB (taper gradually, end quickly)

How do I adjust an audio effect?

1. From the Timeline, select the audio effect you wish to adjust
2. Open the Audio Inspector and select the "Effects" section

3. Click the controls button to the right of the "Effects" section to open a larger window with advanced controls

4. Use these controls to adjust the effect's sound over time or make other edits

How do I turn off or remove an audio effect?

1. To turn an effect off, select the audio effect on the timeline

2. From the Audio Inspector, select the effect and click the corresponding blue checkbox; this will temporarily disable the effect

3. To permanently remove an effect, from the Audio Inspector select the effect and press Delete

How do I move an effect to another clip?

1. Select the effect on the Timeline

2. Go to Edit -> Copy

3. Select the new clip where you wish to apply the effect

4. Go to Edit -> Paste

NOTE: If the original clip had multiple effects associated with it, all of these effects will be copied.

6.3 Correcting audio problems

An ill-timed cough, a plane flying overhead or even the sound of recording equipment can be fixed during post-production using the Audio Enhancement tools. Let's say your problem is the hum of your recording equipment. Here's how to fix it:

1. Select your clip
2. Go to Window -> Show Audio Enhancements
3. In the Hum category, you'll notice that a red warning sign indicates the presence of an electrical hum
4. Remove this hum by clicking the Auto Enhance button at the bottom of the Audio Enhancements Inspector

6.4 Advanced audio editing

How can I use keyframes to manage audio effects?

Keyframes are primary points in a clip that allow you to create basic changes to the audio over the length of the clip. For example, adding a keyframe to the middle of the clip allows you to then automatically fade out the volume or an audio effect based on the location of this keyframe.

1. To get started, first add your keyframe for audio-only: go to the Audio Animation Editor and option click at the point where you wish to add your keyframe
2. Keyframes for volume adjustment appear as white diamonds
3. Drag the keyframes up or down to manually increase or decrease the volume for this specific portion of the clip

How do I increase or lower the overall audio level of my movie while preserving each clip's relative volume?

1. Command + A to select all clips

2. To raise the overall volume one decibel at a time, click Control and +. To lower the overall volume one decibel at a time, click Control and –.

How do I export audio?

Audio can be exported as mono, stereo or surround sound. To export your project as an audio-only file (without the video), do the following:

1. Share -> Export Media
2. Select 'Audio Only' from the pop-up menu
3. Select your audio format: you can choose from AAC, AC3, AIFF, CAF, MP3 or WAVE.
4. Select Compressor if your file is going to be used to continue processing your project's movie for distribution
5. Add a name and select Save

6.5 Syncing audio to video clips

Final Cut Pro X now syncs external audio recorders to DSLR audio files. This is great for users shooting video with the DSLR who use an external microphone to better capture sound, rather than the built-in mic.

1. After importing files, select the video and audio clips you wish to synchronize

2. Right click on the selected clips and choose "Synchronize Clips" from the pop-up menu

3. You will now have a single compound clip

4. Drag the clip to the Timeline or click "Open in Timeline"

5. Play the clip to ensure the sound is properly aligned

6. Next, remove the background audio from the DSLR source file: open the Inspector window, select Audio and uncheck the original source file

7. If you recorded with a shotgun mic, then your audio channel is mono, rather than stereo; to change this, select 'Dual Mono' under Stereos

[7]

COLOR GRADING

7.1 Understanding color basics

If you're shooting without your own lighting team (as most of us are), Final Cut Pro allows you to fix any color issues in postproduction. There are three main ways to enhance color:

- Set Final Cut Pro to automatically color balance clips on import (3.2)
- Match color balance from one clip to another
- Adjust color attributes using Final Cut Pro's Color Board

Before you start tweaking the color of your movie clips, it's helpful to understand a little color theory. Video color uses an additive color system; this means that all the colors, when added together, will equal white. Consequently, achieving "white balance" is extremely important. White balance is affected by your lighting conditions. Shooting indoors, with tungsten or halogen lamps, will produce a different white balance than shooting outside in bright sunlight. When the white balance is off, your colors will also be off. You may even experience a "color cast" on your video, which occurs when too much of one color begins to overwhelm the others. There are three elements of color:

- Hue: The color itself; in videography, there are three primary colors (red, green and blue). When these primary colors are combined, they create the three secondary colors (yellow, magenta and cyan).
- Saturation: The amount of color in an image; 0% saturation is white, 100% is

the original color. For example, red at 50% with be a rose color, 25% will be a soft pink.

- Luminance: The amount of lightness or darkness; 100% luminance is white, 0% luminance is black

7.2 Correcting for color cast

How do I correct for color cast?

Color cast is one of the most common color problems in videography. For example, when shooting indoors, you may have a blue or yellow color cast on your film, depending on your light source.

1. To correct for this, select a clip and then select Video Inspector
2. From the color box, check 'Balance'
3. Once balance is enabled, the color cast will be removed

How can I batch correct for color cast?

If an entire set of clips has color cast issues (even if the problem is slightly different in each clip), you can batch correct, rather than addressing each clip individually.

1. Select the clips you wish to correct in the project by drawing a selection rectangle around the clips
2. Go to Modify -> Color Balance

7.3 Using the Color Board

After automatic color balance is applied, you still may need to tweak the color of individual clips. To do so, you will need to use the Color Board

1. From the Timeline toolbar, select Enhancement -> Show Color Board
2. Once the Color Board is opened, you can edit color (hue), saturation and exposure
3. Open the Video Scopes window to better monitor the results of your color editing; got to Window -> Show Video Scopes
4. We recommend starting with luminance or exposure levels; once the shows, midtones and highlights have been balanced, move on to color and then saturation
5. Use midtones adjustment to add more detail to an image that is underexposed or washed out

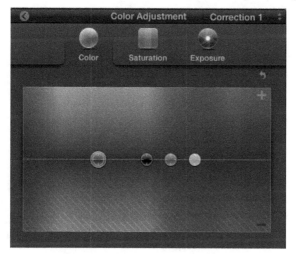

How do I apply the same Color Board changes to all the clips in my project?

Final Cut Pro makes it easy to edit once and then apply these edits to a select group of clips or all your clips. Here's what to do:

1. Select the clips you wish to correct
2. From Color Board select Match Color
3. Skim through clips to choose the source clip
4. Click 'Apply Match'
5. To compare the clip with and without the new color changes, select/deselect the 'Match Color' checkbox

[8]

TRANSITIONS

8.1 Transitions

This effect is added between clips and controls how one clip changes (transitions) into the next. Popular transitions include fades, swipes and cross dissolves. Transitions can fade in, fade out, or be part of a crossfade where the previous video or audio fades down as the new video/audio fades up.

NOTE: *When a transition effect is added to a video clip with attached audio, a crossfade will be automatically applied to both. If the audio is* detached from the video, then the audio will not be affected.

How do I add the cross dissolve transition?

1. To add a cross dissolve to the end or beginning of a clip, use the select tool and click the clip's edge
2. To add a cross dissolve to both ends of the clip, select the entire clip
3. Choose Edit -> Add Cross Dissolve or use the keyboard shortcut Command + T
4. If the video clip has attached audio, a cross fade transition will be applied to the audio

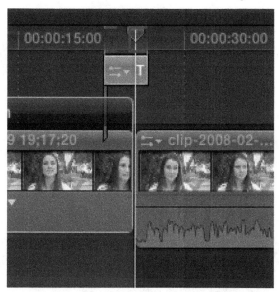

How do I add a transition with the Transitions Browser?

1. Select the Transitions browser from the Toolbar
2. Select your desired transition
3. Click and drag your transition to an edit point in the clip
4. To replace an existing transition, simply drag a new one to it

8.2 Titles

Need to roll the credits? Add text to set up a scene? Use Titles to add text to any clip in your project.

How do I add a title to a project clip?

1. Position the playhead on the Timeline where you wish to add your title
2. Select the Title browser from the Toolbar

3. Double click on any title; it will be added to the playhead position on your Timeline

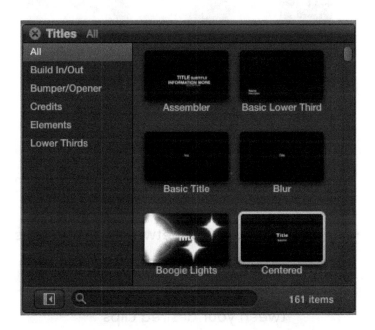

How do I edit the text in my title?

1. Select your new title from the Timeline

2. From the Viewer, click on the 'title' placeholder text

3. Type in the new text for your title

4. You can change the text position by clicking and dragging it to new locations

How do I add a title as its own clip to the Time-line?

- To add a title between existing clips, simply drag your selected title from the Title browser and position it between your desired clips

- To replace an existing title, select your replacement title from the Title browser, drag it to the old title on your Timeline, and choose Replace

8.3 Effects

Add a variety of effects to your video clips, ranging from subtitles to dream sequences.

- Built-in effects are standard effects that allow you to resize, move, rotate, trim and apply the Ken Burns zooming effect. These effects are 'built-in' and already part of each Timeline clip – all you need to do is activate an effect and adjust it.

- Clip effects change your video to create dream sequence, film grain, special colors, etc.

Many of these effects, along with generators, can be opened in Motion. This is an Apple application specifically created to work with Final Cut Pro. If you need to customize an effect or save specialized versions of an effect, you will need to use Motion. The latest version of Motion was completely redesigned in conjunction with Final Cut Pro X to also take advantage of 64-bit processing, Grand Central Dispatch, Cocoa and a shared render engine for peak performance and quality with Final Cut Pro and Compressor.

How do I add a built-in effect?

Built-in effects can be used to create a composited image, reposition a clip by zooming in on a subject or crop a clip to remove unwanted items.

1. Select a clip on the Timeline
2. Many built-in effects can be accessed from the lower-left of the Viewer
3. For example, to crop a clip, select the crop tool and use the blue handles to adjust the crop ratio; clicking 'done' will apply the effect and resize the cropped image to fit the window

How do I animate a built-in effect?

Animating a built-in effect, like cropping, can replicate a pan-and-zoom camera – even if you were just using your iPhone to capture the image.

1. To animate a built-in effect, add a Keyframe to the start of the clip
2. Move the playhead to the end of the clip and use the effect's controls to adjust the end position; a second keyframe will be automatically added

3. When you are finished, click "Done" in the upper right of the Viewer

4. When you play the clip, Final Cut Pro will move smoothly between the two keyframes, animating the effect

How do I add the Ken Burns effect?

Ken Burns, the documentary filmmaker, is famous for his pan and zoom effect. In Final Cut Pro, the Ken Burns effect uses two cropped stills – one at the beginning and one at the end – to create the pan and zoom effect. (This is different than the animation discussed above, as this only uses cropping at either the beginning or end of a clip, never both)

1. Select a clip on the Timeline

2. Activate the Ken Burns effect by right clicking on the crop button

3. Two rectangles now appear in the viewer; the green one defines the start position and the red one defines the end position; a super-imposed arrow defines the direction of movement

4. To resize or move the rectangles, click and drag their handles; to switch between rectangles, click either the green start or the red finish labels

5. To switch the start and finish rectangles, click "Swap" at the top of the Viewer

6. When you are finished, click "Done" in the upper right corner of the Viewer

How do I add a clip effect?

Add a dream sequence, switch to black and white, or make your clip glow. With Final Cut Pro's clip effect library, these changes are as easy as a few clicks of your mouse.

1. Select a clip on the Timeline

2. Select the "Effects" button on the Toolbar

3. From the Effects browser, select your desired effect

4. You can preview this effect by moving the pointer over the effect's thumbnails

5. To apply the effect, either drag and drop the effect on your Timeline, or double click the effect from the Effects browser

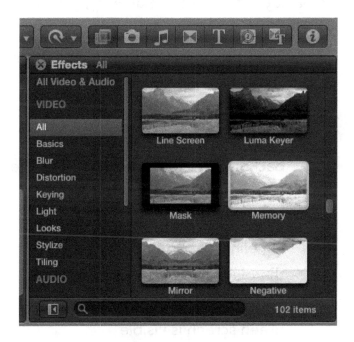

How do I key one clip over another?

Keying allows you to combine two clips to create one single image, such as super imposing an actor filmed against a green screen with a dramatic mountaintop background. During the keying process, the foreground clip (also known as the top clip) is processed to eliminate color (chroma keying) or luma values (luma keying) so that it can be combined with the bottom clip.

Chroma keys are uses for managing green screen:

1. Drag the primary clip (with the green screen) to the Timeline; this is the Foreground
2. Drag the secondary clip (with the backdrop) to the Timeline; this is the Background
3. Select the foreground clip on the Timeline; for optimal keying, positing the play head at the point in the Foreground clip where the most green screen is visible
4. Click the Effects button on the toolbar and then select the 'Keyer' effect from the effects browser
5. Double click the Keyer effect to apply it to the selected clip.
6. The Keyer effect will automatically analyze the clip to detect the primary

color (a vibrant green or blue) and remove this color

Luma keys are used for adding a logo or computer-generated graphic over a dark background.

1. From the Timeline, select your background clip and drag the playhead to the point where you wish to begin superimposing the luma clip
2. From the Event Browser, select the foreground clip and select Edit -> Connect to Primary Storyline
3. Select the Effects button and select the 'Luma Keyer' effect
4. Double click to apply the effect to the selected foreground clip
5. The Luma Keyer effect will remove the black video

8.4 Generators

Generators are special elements, like a Timecode counter or background, which can be added to a project. Generators, like effects, can be customized using Motion.

How do I add a Timecode counter?

1. Select the desired clip
2. Open the Generators Browser from the toolbar
3. Select the Timecode generator and drag to place on the clip
4. Use the Generator inspector to configure the Timecode settings

How do I select a background for adding built-in effects?

1. Position the playhead at the point on the Timeline where you wish to add the background
2. Open the Generators Browser from the toolbar
3. Select your desired background clip
4. Use the Generators inspector to configure the background, as needed

[9]

EXPORTING AND SHARING

9.1 Preparing for export: correcting audio levels and brightness

To the human ear and eye, audio and visuals may look and sound perfect, but there may be underlying trouble spots. For example, in digital audio distortion occurs when the combined audio level of all clips exceeds zero dB. As a rule of thumb, primary audio should peak at -12 dB, and any background audio should peak at -18dB. The overall combined level should never exceed -6dB. High luminosity levels are a common visual video problem. The FCC mandates that all videos intended for broadcast never exceed a luminance level over 100 IRE (100%).

Before you export your project, use Final Cut to check for problems with volume and luminosity.

To check for volume control:
1. View the audio meters pane while watching playback
2. Activate audio meters by clicking on the right side of the dashboard
3. From the timeline, look for red or yellow tipped sound waves
4. Right click on the volume control line to create keyframes; adjust the specific section of the clip

To check for broadcast-safe luminosity levels:

1. From the Effects Browser, select the "Broadcast Safe" effect
2. When activated, this effect will automatically adjust the luminance of the entire clip

9.2 Export project as movie file with video and audio

1. Select your project from the Project Library
2. Go to Share -> Export Media

3. Select "Video and Audio" from the pop-up menu
4. Select the Video codec (choose from Apple ProRes, H.264, and uncompressed 8- and 10-bit 4:2:2)
5. Click 'Summary' to check output details
6. Select location for your file and click save

]*What happens if I see a "missing media content" dialog?*

You may see this error message if there is a problem with your Event References. This happens when you import audio or video, and the imported content becomes disconnected from the original file. Here's what to do:

1. Go to Project Library; you should see a red background and yellow alert flag where content is missing
2. Go to the Properties dialog (upper right) and select Modify Event References
3. You can now reconnect your clips with their original location on the hard drive or external drive

You can also use the "relink" feature available in Final Cut 10.0.3. To do this, be sure that you are using the latest version released in January 2012 or later, as relink was not included in the initial Final Cut X release:

1. Right click the Event Library with the missing media
2. Choose "Relink Event Files"

9.3 Publishing to an Apple Device

You can publish your movie directly to an iPhone, iPad, Apple TV, Mac or PC:

1. Choose Share -> Apple Devices
2. Select the desired output
3. To see how your movie will look on each device, select a device and skim the video screen; this is helpful for identifying compatibility issues between different devices
4. Check the "Add to iTunes" default option
5. Select the final size; the movie will be encoded and formatted for maximum compatibility and quality
6. When you export files for "high quality", be aware that the sizes can be very large; confirm that your drive has room prior to exporting
7. If there is a problem rendering a file, the "share" icon will pop up allowing you to check for error information

You can also publish directly to an iLife or iWork app, such as Garage Band or Keynote. Simply select Share -> Media Browser. Publishing will make your movie accessible in the media browser of these applications.

9.4 Sending to Compressor

Compressor is a professional transcoding application that was built specifically to work with Final Cut Pro. Compressor gives users full control media-conversion specifications. If you have Compressor installed on your computer, you can send your project directly to Compressor. This allows you to create highly customized settings, such as adding a watermark to your video.

1. To send your project to compressor:
2. Select the project
3. Go to Share -> Send to Compressor
4. Compressor will open a new batch based on your project's media

CONCLUSION

Final Cut Pro truly redefines post-production for professionals, and makes it easy for the amateur filmmaker to upgrade from iMovie. If you are switching from Final Cut 7, it may take a few uses to become comfortable with the new Final Cut Pro X interface and workflow. Remember, Final Cut X is not an upgrade, but a completely new application. Once you are up to speed, it's easy to see how Final Cut Pro X is a powerful production tool. From customizing Keystrokes to unlocking full editing potential with advanced transitions, generators and sound effects, Final Cut Pro X will take your movies to the next level and beyond.

This guide covered many of the "getting started" basics, smoothed the transition from Final Cut 7 to X, and also included advanced editing tips for managing audio, transitions and other special effects. For continued support with advanced editing and user tips, be sure to visit Apple's online support forums. (https://discussions.apple.com/community/professional_applications/final_cut_pro_x)